The Arraignment of Paris by George Peele

A PASTORALL

Presented before the Queenes Maiestie, by the Children of her Chappell

Performed c. 1581. First Published 1584

George Peele was born in July 1556 and baptised on the 25th at St James Garlickhythe in the City of London.

A completely accurate record of his life is not possible but enough accounts and records exist to provide some background.

His father, James was a clerk at Christ's Hospital, then a central London school, and authored two treatises on bookkeeping.

Peele himself was initially educated at Christ's Hospital before entering Broadgates Hall, Oxford, in 1571. Three years after in 1574 he moved to Christ Church and took his B.A. there in 1577, and then his M.A. in 1579. Something appears to have so upset the Governors that they requested their clerk to 'discharge his house of his son, George Peele.'

His mother, Anne, died on July 1st, 1580, and his father remarried to Christian Widers, a nurse at the hospital a few months later.

Peele himself appears to have married, around this time, Ann Cooke, a heiress. He appears to have been rather reckless with her assets and they were soon gone.

What he did appear to be hard at work on was his writing. His pastoral comedy 'The Arraignment of Paris' was presented by the Children of the Chapel Royal before Queen Elizabeth perhaps by 1581, and was printed anonymously in 1584.

He was praised in 1585 for his translation from the Greek of one of the 'Iphigenias of Euripides'. That same year, 1585, he was employed to write the 'Device of the Pageant', and in 1591 he devised a pageant in honour of another Lord Mayor, Sir William Webbe. This was the 'Descensus Astraeae', in which Queen Elizabeth is honoured as Astraea.

Much of the rest of his life is not certain and various facts, accounts and information is in dispute.

He may have married for a second time but what happened to Ann is not recorded. He was also awarded the authorship of several plays many of which have now fallen away although modern research methods. However, knowing the collaboration between many of the dramatists of that time his hand has been detected and confirmed in some other plays.

Perhaps the most famous of these is Shakespeare's 'Titus Andronicus'. It is now thought that Peele wrote the first act as well as the first two scenes in Act II, with Shakespeare responsible for the rest. The exact measure of each is difficult to ascertain any further.

As a writer he is acknowledged to be one of the era's finest and ranked alongside Marlowe, Spenser, and Shakespeare.

The other plays for which Peele can reliably be given authorship are 'Edward I', (printed 1593) 'The Old Wives' Tale', 'The Battle of Alcazar' (printed 1594) and David and Bethsabe (printed 1599). 'The Troublesome Reign of John, King of England', the immediate source for Shakespeare's King John, has been published under Peele's name.

George Peel died, accounts say of the pox, and was buried on the 9th November 1596 in St James's Church, Clerkenwell.

Index of Contents

DRAMATIS PERSONAE

The Olympian Gods and Goddesses:
Jupiter, king of all the gods
Juno, queen of the gods
Apollo, god of music, medicine and the sun
Bacchus, god of wine and revelry
Diana, goddess of hunting and chastity
Mars, god of war
Mercury, Jupiter's messenger
Neptune, ruler of the seas
Pallas, goddess of war and wisdom
Pluto, ruler of the underworld
Venus, goddess of beauty
Vulcan, the blacksmith
Minor Gods and Goddesses:
Pan, god of flocks and herdsman
Faunus, god of fields
Silvanus, god of forests
Saturn, god of agriculture
Pomona, goddess of orchards and gardens
Flora, goddess of flowers and gardens
Ate, goddess of discord
Clotho, one of the Fates
Lachesis, one of the Fates
Atropos, one of the Fates
The Muses, protectors of the arts
A Nymph of Diana
Rhanis, a nymph
Mortals:
Paris, a shepherd, son of King Priam of Troy
Colin, a shepherd
Hobbinol, a shepherd
Diggon, a shepherd
Thenot, a shepherd
Oenone
Helen
Thestylis
Cupids, Cyclops, Shepherds, Knights, &c.

SCENE:—The entire play takes place in the valleys and woods of Mt. Ida, near Troy, in Asia Minor

THE ARRAIGNMENT OF PARIS

Enter **ATÉ**

Condemnèd soul, Até, from lowest hell,
And deadly rivers of th' infernal Jove,
Where bloodless ghosts in pains of endless date
Fill ruthless ears with never-ceasing cries,
Behold, I come in place, and bring beside
The bane of Troy! behold, the fatal fruit,
Raught from the golden tree of Proserpine!
Proud Troy must fall, so bid the gods above,
And stately Ilium's lofty towers be racet
By conquering hands of the victorious foe;
King Priam's palace waste with flaming fire,
Whose thick and foggy smoke, piercing the sky,
Must serve for messenger of sacrifice,
T' appease the anger of the angry heavens;
And Priam's younger son, the shepherd swain,
Paris, th' unhappy organ of the Greeks.
So, loth and weary of her heavy load,
The Earth complains unto the hellish prince,
Surcharged with the burden that she nill sustain.
Th' unpartial daughters of Necessity
Bin aidès in her suit: and so the twine
That holds old Priam's house, the thread of Troy,
Dame Atropos with knife in sunder cuts.
Done be the pleasure of the powers above,
Whose hests men must obey: and I my part
Perform in Ida vales. Lordings, adieu;
Imposing silence for your task, I end,
Till just assembly of the goddesses
Make me begin the tragedy of Troy.

[Exit **ATÉ** cum aureo pomo.

ACT I

SCENE I

PAN, **FAUNUS**, and **SILVANUS**, with their **ATTENDANTS**, enter to give welcome to the goddesses: Pan's **SHEPHERD** has a lamb, Faunus' **HUNTER** has a fawn, and Silvanus' **WOODMAN** with an oaken-bough laden with acorns.

PAN
Silvanus, either Flora doth us wrong,

Or Faunus made us tarry all too long,
For by this morning mirth it should appear,
The Muses or the goddesses be near.

FAUNUS
My fawn was nimble, Pan, and whipt apace, –
'Twas happy that we caught him up at last, –
The fattest, fairest fawn in all the chace;
I wonder how the knave could skip so fast.

PAN
And I have brought a twagger for the nones,
A bunting lamb; nay, pray you, feel no bones:
Believe me now my cunning much I miss,
If ever Pan felt fatter lamb than this.

SILVANUS
Sirs, you may boast your flocks and herds that bin both fresh and fair,
Yet hath Silvanus walks, i-wis, that stand in wholesome air;
And, lo, the honour of the woods, the gallant oaken-bough,
Do I bestow, laden with acorns and with mast enow!

PAN
Peace, man, for shame! shalt have both lambs and dames and flocks and herds and all,
And all my pipes to make the glee; we meet not now to brawl.

FAUNUS
There's no such matter. Pan; we are all friends assembled hether.
To bid Queen Juno and her feres most humbly welcome hether:
Diana, mistress of our woods, her presence will not want;
Her courtesy to all her friends, we wot, is nothing scant.

SCENE II

Enter **POMONA** with her fruit.

POMONA
Yea, Pan, no farther yet, and had the start of me?
Why, then, Pomona with her fruit comes time enough, I see.
Come on a while; with country store, like friends, we venture forth:
Think'st, Faunus, that these goddesses will take our gifts in worth?

FAUNUS
Yea, doubtless, for shall tell thee, dame, 'twere better give a thing,
A sign of love, unto a mighty person or a king,
Than to a rude and barbarous swain, but bad and basely born,

For gently takes the gentleman that oft the clown will scorn.

PAN
Say'st truly, Faunus; I myself have given good tidy lambs
To Mercury, may say to thee, to Phoebus, and to Jove;
When to a country mops, forsooth, chave offered all their dams,
And piped and prayed for little worth, and ranged about the grove.

POMONA
God Pan, that makes your flock so thin, and makes you look so lean,
To kiss in corners.

PAN
Well said, wench! some other thing you mean.

POMONA
Yea, jest it out till it go alone: but marvel where we miss
Fair Flora all this merry morn.

FAUNUS
Some news; see where she is.

SCENE III

Enter **FLORA** to the country gods.

PAN
Flora, well met, and for thy taken pain,
Poor country gods, thy debtors we remain.

FLORA
Believe me, Pan, not all thy lambs and yoes,
Nor, Faunus, all thy lusty bucks and does,
(But that I am instructed well to know
What service to the hills and dales I owe,)
Could have enforced me to so strange a toil,
Thus to enrich this gaudy, gallant soil.

FAUNUS
But tell me, wench, hast done't so trick indeed,
That heaven itself may wonder at the deed?

FLORA
Not Iris, in her pride and bravery,
Adorns her arch with such variety;
Nor doth the milk-white way, in frosty night,

Appear so fair and beautiful in sight,
As done these fields, and groves, and sweetest bowers,
Bestrewed and decked with parti-coloured flowers,
Along the bubbling brooks and silver glide,
That at the bottom doth in silence slide;
The watery-flowers and lilies on the banks,
Like blazing comets, burgen all in ranks;
Under the hawthorn and the poplar-tree,
Where sacred Phoebe may delight to be,
The primrose, and the purple hyacinth,
The dainty violet, and the wholesome minth,
The double daisy, and the cowslip, queen
Of summer flowers, do overpeer the green;
And round about the valley as ye pass,
Ye may ne see for peeping flowers the grass:
That well the mighty Juno, and the rest,
May boldly think to be a welcome guest
On Ida hills, when to approve the thing,
The Queen of Flowers prepares a second spring.

SILVANUS
Thou gentle nymph, what thanks shall we repay
To thee that mak'st our fields and woods so gay?

FLORA
Silvanus, when it is thy hap to see
My workmanship in portraying all the three,
First stately Juno with her port and grace,
Her robes, her lawns, her crownet, and her mace,
Would make thee muse this picture to behold,
Of yellow oxlips bright as burnished gold.

POMONA
A rare device; and Flora well, perdy,
Did paint her yellow for her jealousy.

FLORA
Pallas in flowers of hue and colours red;
Her plumes, her helm, her lance, her Gorgon's head,
Her trailing tresses that hang flaring round,
Of July-flowers so graffèd in the ground,
That, trust me, sirs, who did the cunning see,
Would at a blush suppose it to be she.

PAN
Good Flora, by my flock, 'twere very good
To dight her all in red resembling blood.

FLORA

Fair Venus of sweet violets in blue,
With other flowers infixed for change of hue;
Her plumes, her pendants, bracelets, and her rings.
Her dainty fan, and twenty other things,
Her lusty mantle waving in the wind,
And every part in colour and in kind;
And for her wreath of roses, she nill dare
With Flora's cunning counterfeit compare.
So that what living wight shall chance to see
These goddesses, each placed in her degree,
Portrayed by Flora's workmanship alone,
Must say that art and nature met in one.

SILVANUS

A dainty draught to lay her down in blue,
The colour commonly betokening true.

FLORA

This piece of work, compact with many a flower,
And well laid in at entrance of the bower,
Where Phoebe means to make this meeting royal,
Have I prepared to welcome them withal.

POMONA

And are they yet dismounted, Flora, say.
That we may wend to meet them on the way?

FLORA

That shall not need: they are at hand by this,
And the conductor of the train hight Rhanis.
Juno hath left her chariot long ago,
And hath returned her peacocks by her rainbow;
And bravely, as becomes the wife of Jove,
Doth honour by her presence to our grove.
Fair Venus she hath let her sparrows fly,
To tend on her and make her melody;
Her turtles and her swans unyokèd be.
And flicker near her side for company.
Pallas hath set her tigers loose to feed,
Commanding them to wait when she hath need.
And hitherward with proud and stately pace,
To do us honour in the sylvan chace,
They march, like to the pomp of heaven above,
Juno the wife and sister of King Jove,
The warlike Pallas, and the Queen of Love.

PAN

Pipe, Pan, for joy, and let thy shepherds sing;
Shall never age forget this memorable thing.

FLORA
Clio, the sagest of the Sisters Nine,
To do observance to this dame divine,
Lady of learning and of chivalry,
Is here arrived in fair assembly,
And wandering up and down th' unbeaten ways,
Ring through the wood sweet songs of Pallas' praise.

POMONA
Hark, Flora, Faunus! here is melody,
A charm of birds, and more than ordinary.

[An artificial charm of birds being heard within.

PAN
The silly birds make mirth; then should we do them wrong,
Pomona, if we nill bestow an echo to their song.

[**THE SONG.**

[A quire within and without.

GODS
O Ida, O Ida, O Ida, happy hill!
This honour done to Ida may it continue still!

MUSES [Within]
Ye country gods that in this Ida won,
Bring down your gifts of welcome,
For honour done to Ida.

GODS
Behold, in sign of joy we sing.
And signs of joyful welcome bring.
For honour done to Ida.

MUSES [Within]
The Muses give you melody to gratulate this chance,
And Phoebe, chief of sylvan chace, commands you all to dance.

GODS
Then round in a circle our sportance must be,
Hold hands in a hornpipe, all gallant in glee.

[Dance.

MUSES [Within]
Reverence, reverence, most humble reverence!

GODS
Most humble reverence!

JUNO, **PALLAS** and **VENUS** enter, **RHANIS** leading the way. **PAN** alone sings.

[**THE SONG**.
The God of Shepherds, and his mates,
With country cheer salutes your states,
Fair, wise, and worthy as you be.
And thank the gracious ladies three
For honour done to Ida.

[The **BIRDS** sing.

[The song being done, **JUNO** speaks.

JUNO
Venus, what shall I say? for, though I be a dame divine,
This welcome and this melody exceed these wits of mine.

VENUS
Believe me, Juno, as I hight the Sovereign of Love,
These rare delights in pleasures pass the banquets of King Jove.

PALLAS
Then, Venus, I conclude, it easily may be seen,
That in her chaste and pleasant walks fair Phoebe is a queen.

RHANIS
Divine Pallas, and you sacred dames,
Juno and Venus, honoured by your names,
Juno, the wife and sister of King Jove,
Fair Venus, lady-president of love,
If any entertainment in this place,
That can afford but homely, rude, and base,
It please your godheads to accept in gree,
That gracious thought our happiness shall be.
My mistress Dian, this right well I know,
For love that to this presence she doth owe,
Accounts more honour done to her this day,

Than ever whilom in these woods of Ida;
And for our country gods, I dare be bold,
They make such cheer, your presence to behold,
Such jouisance, such mirth, and merriment,
As nothing else their mind might more content:
And that you do believe it to be so,
Fair goddesses, your lovely looks do show.
It rests in fine, for to confirm my talk,
Ye deign to pass along to Dian's walk;
Where she among her troop of maids attends
The fair arrival of her welcome friends.

FLORA
And we will wait with all observance due,
And do just honour to this heavenly crew.

PAN
The God of Shepherds, Juno, ere thou go,
Intends a lamb on thee for to bestow.

FAUNUS
Faunus, high ranger in Diana's chace.
Presents a fawn to Lady Venus' grace.

SILVANUS
Silvanus gives to Pallas' deity
This gallant bough raught from the oaken-tree.

POMONA
To them that do this honour to our fields,
Her mellow apples poor Pomona yields.

JUNO
And, gentle gods, these signs of your goodwill
We take in worth, and shall accept them still.

VENUS
And, Flora, this to thee among the rest, –
Thy workmanship comparing with the best,
Let it suffice thy cunning to have [power]
To call King Jove from forth his heavenly bower.
Hadst thou a lover, Flora, credit me,
I think thou wouldst bedeck him gallantly.
But wend we on; and, Rhanis, lead the way,
That kens the painted paths of pleasant Ida.

[Exeunt.

Enter **PARIS** and **OENONE**.

PARIS
Oenone, while we bin disposed to walk.
Tell me what shall be subject of our talk?
Thou hast a sort of pretty tales in store,
Dare say no nymph in Ida woods hath more:
Again, beside thy sweet alluring face,
In telling them thou hast a special grace.
Then, prithee, sweet, afford some pretty thing,
Some toy that from thy pleasant wit doth spring.

OENONE
Paris, my heart's contentment and my choice,
Use thou thy pipe, and I will use my voice;
So shall thy just request not be denied,
And time well spent, and both be satisfied.

PARIS
Well, gentle nymph, although thou do me wrong,
That can ne tune my pipe unto a song,
Me list this once, Oenone, for thy sake.
This idle task on me to undertake.
They sit under a tree together.

OENONE
And whereon, then, shall be my roundelay?
For thou hast heard my store long since, dare say;
How Saturn did divide his kingdom tho
To Jove, to Neptune, and to Dis below;
How mighty men made foul successless war
Against the gods and state of Jupiter;
How Phorcys' imp, that was so trick and fair,
That tangled Neptune in her golden hair,
Became a Gorgon for her lewd misdeed, –
A pretty fable, Paris, for to read,
A piece of cunning, trust me, for the nones,
That wealth and beauty alter men to stones;
How Salmacis, resembling idleness,
Turns men to women all through wantonness;
How Pluto caught Queen Ceres' daughter thence,
And what did follow of that love-offence;
Of Daphne turned into the laurel-tree,
That shows a mirror of virginity;

How fair Narcissus tooting on his shade,
Reproves disdain, and tells how form doth vade;
How cunning Philomela's needle tells
What force in love, what wit in sorrow dwells;
What pains unhappy souls abide in hell,
They say because on earth they lived not well, –
Ixion's wheel, proud Tantal's pining woe,
Prometheus' torment, and a many mo.
How Danaus' daughters ply their endless task,
What toil the toil of Sisyphus doth ask:
All these are old and known I know, yet, if thou wilt have any,
Choose some of these, for, trust me, else Oenone hath not many.

PARIS
Nay, what thou wilt: but sith my cunning not compares with thine,
Begin some toy that I can play upon this pipe of mine.

OENONE
There is a pretty sonnet, then, we call it Cupid's Curse,
"They that do change old love for new, pray gods they change for worse!"
The note is fine and quick withal, the ditty will agree,
Paris, with that same vow of thine upon our poplar-tree.

PARIS
No better thing; begin it, then: Oenone, thou shalt see
Our music figure of the love that grows 'twixt thee and me.

[They sing; and while **OENONE** sings, he pipes.

OENONE
Fair and fair, and twice so fair,
As fair as any may be;
The fairest shepherd on our green,
A love for any lady.

PARIS
Fair and fair, and twice so fair,
As fair as any may be;
Thy love is fair for thee alone,
And for no other lady.

OENONE
My love is fair, my love is gay,
As fresh as bin the flowers in May,
And of my love my roundelay,
My merry merry merry roundelay,
Concludes with Cupid's curse, –
They that do change old love for new.

Pray gods they change for worse!
Ambo. Simul. They that do change, &c.

OENONE
Fair and fair, &c.

PARIS
Fair and fair, &c.
Thy love is fair, &c

OENONE
My love can pipe, my love can sing.
My love can many a pretty thing,
And of his lovely praises ring
My merry merry roundelays,
Amen to Cupid's curse, –
They that do change, &c.

PARIS
They that do change, &c.

BOTH
Fair and fair, &c.

[The song being ended, they rise.

OENONE
Sweet shepherd, for Oenone's sake be cunning in this song,
And keep thy love, and love thy choice, or else thou dost her wrong.

PARIS
My vow is made and witnessèd, the poplar will not start,
Nor shall the nymph Oenone's love from forth my breathing heart.
I will go bring thee on thy way, my flock are here behind,
And I will have a lover's fee; they say, unkissed unkind.

[Exeunt.

ACT II

SCENE I

Enter **JUNO**, **PALLAS** and **VENUS**.

VENUS [Ex-abrupto]
But pray you, tell me, Juno, was it so,

As Pallas told me here the tale of Echo?

JUNO
She was a nymph indeed, as Pallas tells,
A walker, such as in these thickets dwells;
And as she told what subtle juggling pranks
She played with Juno, so she told her thanks:
A tattling trull to come at every call,
And now, forsooth, nor tongue nor life at all.
And though perhaps she was a help to Jove,
And held me chat while he might court his love,
Believe me, dames, I am of this opinion,
He took but little pleasure in the minion;
And whatsoe'er his scapes have been beside,
Dare say for him, 'a never strayed so wide:
A lovely nut-brown lass or lusty trull
Have power perhaps to make a god a bull.

VENUS
Gramercy, gentle Juno, for that jest;
I' faith, that item was worth all the rest.

PALLAS
No matter, Venus, howsoe'er you scorn,
My father Jove at that time ware the horn.

JUNO
Had every wanton god above, Venus, not better luck,
Then heaven would be a pleasant park, and Mars a lusty buck.

VENUS
Tut, Mars hath horns to butt withal, although no bull 'a shows,
'A never needs to mask in nets, 'a fears no jealous froes.

JUNO
Forsooth, the better is his turn, for, if 'a speak too loud,
Must find some shift to shadow him, a net or else a cloud.

PALLAS
No more of this, fair goddesses; unrip not so your shames,
To stand all naked to the world, that bene such heavenly dames.

JUNO
Nay, Pallas, that's a common trick with Venus well we know,
And all the gods in heaven have seen her naked long ago.

VENUS
And then she was so fair and bright, and lovely and so trim,

As Mars is but for Venus' tooth, and she will sport with him:
And, but me list not here to make comparison with Jove,
Mars is no ranger, Juno, he, in every open grove.

PALLAS
Too much of this: we wander far, the skies begin to scowl;
Retire we to Diana's bower, the weather will be foul.

[A storm of thunder and lightning passes.

[**ATÉ** trundles the ball into place, crying "Fatum Trojae," **JUNO** takes it up.

JUNO
Pallas, the storm is past and gone, and Phoebus clears the skies,
And, lo, behold a ball of gold, a fair and worthy prize!

[**VENUS** examines the ball closely.

VENUS
This posy wills the apple to the fairest given be;
Then is it mine, for Venus hight the fairest of the three.

PALLAS
The fairest here, as fair is meant, am I, ye do me wrong;
And if the fairest have it must, to me it doth belong.

JUNO
Then Juno may it not enjoy, so every one says no,
But I will prove myself the fairest, ere I lose it so.

[They read the posy.

The brief is this, "Detur pulcherrimae,
Let this unto the fairest given be,
The fairest of the three," – and I am she.

PALLAS
"Detur pulcherrimoe,
Let this unto the fairest given be.
The fairest of the three," – and I am she.

VENUS
"Detur pulcherrimoe,
Let this unto the fairest given be,
The fairest of the three," – and I am she.

JUNO
My face is fair; but yet the majesty,

That all the gods in heaven have seen in me,
Have made them choose me, of the planets seven.
To be the wife of Jove and queen of heaven.
If, then, this prize be but bequeathed to beauty,
The only she that wins this prize am I.

VENUS

That Venus is the fairest, this doth prove,
That Venus is the lovely Queen of Love:
The name of Venus is indeed but beauty,
And men me fairest call per excellency.
If, then, this prize be but bequeathed to beauty,
The only she that wins this prize am I.

PALLAS

To stand on terms of beauty as you take it,
Believe me, ladies, is but to mistake it.
The beauty that this subtle prize must win,
No outward beauty hight, but dwells within;
And sift it as you please, and you shall find,
This beauty is the beauty of the mind:
This fairness, virtue hight in general,
That many branches hath in speciäl;
This beauty wisdom hight, whereof am I,
By heaven appointed, goddess worthily.
And look how much the mind, the better part,
Doth overpass the body in desert,
So much the mistress of those gifts divine
Excels thy beauty, and that state of thine.
Then, if this prize be thus bequeathed to beauty,
The only she that wins this prize am I.

VENUS

Nay, Pallas, by your leave you wander clean:
We must not conster hereof as you mean,
But take the sense as it is plainly meant;
And let the fairest ha't, I am content.

PALLAS

Our reasons will be infinite, I trow,
Unless unto some other point we grow:
But first here's none, methinks, disposed to yield,
And none but will with words maintain the field.

JUNO

Then, if you will, t' avoid a tedious grudge,
Refer it to the sentence of a judge;
Whoe'er he be that cometh next in place,

Let him bestow the ball and end the case.

VENUS
So can it not go wrong with me at all.

PALLAS
I am agreed, however it befall:
And yet by common doom, so may it be,
I may be said the fairest of the three.

JUNO
Then yonder, lo, that shepherd swain is he,
That must be umpire in this controversy!

SCENE II

Enter **PARIS**.

VENUS
Juno, in happy time, I do accept the man;
It seemeth by his looks some skill of love he can.

PARIS [Aside]
The nymph is gone, and I, all solitary,
Must wend to tend my charge, oppressed with melancholy.
This day (or else me fails my shepherd's skill)
Will tide me passing good or passing ill.

JUNO
Shepherd, abash not, though at sudden thus
Thou be arrived by ignorance among us,
Not earthly but divine, and goddesses all three;
Juno, Pallas, Venus, these our titles be.
Nor fear to speak for reverence of the place,
Chosen to end a hard and doubtful case.
This apple, lo (nor ask thou whence it came),
Is to be given unto the fairest dame!
And fairest is, nor she, nor she, but she
Whom, shepherd, thou shalt fairest name to be.
This is thy charge; fulfil without offence,
And she that wins shall give thee recompense.

PALLAS
Dread not to speak, for we have chosen thee,
Sith in this case we can no judges be.

VENUS

And, shepherd, say that I the fairest am,
And thou shalt win good guerdon for the same.

JUNO

Nay, shepherd, look upon my stately grace,
Because the pomp that 'longs to Juno's mace
Thou mayst not see; and think Queen Juno's name,
To whom old shepherds title works of fame,
Is mighty, and may easily suffice,
At Phoebus hand, to gain a golden prize.
And for thy meed, sith I am queen of riches,
Shepherd, I will reward thee with great monarchies,
Empires, and kingdoms, heaps of massy gold,
Sceptres and diadems curious to behold,
Rich robes, of sumptuous workmanship and cost,
And thousand things whereof I make no boast:
The mould whereon thou tread'st shall be of Tagus' sands,
And Xanthus shall run liquid gold for thee to wash thy hands;
And if thou like to tend thy flock, and not from them to fly,
Their fleeces shall be curlèd gold to please their master's eye;
And last, to set thy heart on fire, give this one fruit to me,
And, shepherd, lo, this tree of gold will I bestow on thee!

JUNO'S SHOW.

[A tree of gold rises, laden with diadems and crowns of gold.

The ground whereon it grows, the grass, the root of gold,
The body and the bark of gold, all glistering to behold,
The leaves of burnished gold, the fruits that thereon grow
Are diadems set with pearl in gold, in gorgeous glistering show;
And if this tree of gold in lieu may not suffice,
Require a grove of golden trees, so Juno bear the prize.

[The tree sinks.

PALLAS

Me list not tempt thee with decaying wealth,
Which is embased by want of lusty health;
But if thou have a mind to fly above,
Y-crowned with fame, near to the seat of Jove,
If thou aspire to wisdom's worthiness,
Whereof thou mayst not see the brightness,
If thou desire honour of chivalry,
To be renowned for happy victory,
To fight it out, and in the champaign field
To shroud thee under Pallas' warlike shield,

To prance on barbèd steeds, this honour, lo,
Myself for guerdon shall on thee bestow!
And for encouragement, that thou mayst see
What famous knights Dame Pallas' warriors be,
Behold in Pallas' honour here they come,
Marching along with sound of thundering drum.

PALLAS' SHOW.

[Enter **NINE KNIGHTS** in armour, treading a warlike almain, by drum and fife; and then they having marched forth again, VENUS speaks.

VENUS
Come, shepherd, come, sweet shepherd, look on me.
These bene too hoat alarums these for thee:
But if thou wilt give me the golden ball,
Cupid my boy shall ha't to play withal,
That, whensoe'er this apple he shall see,
The God of Love himself shall think on thee.
And bid thee look and choose, and he will wound
Whereso thy fancy's object shall be found;
And lightly when he shoots, he doth not miss:
And I will give thee many a lovely kiss.
And come and play with thee on Ida here;
And if thou wilt a face that hath no peer,
A gallant girl, a lusty minion trull,
That can give sport to thee thy bellyfull,
To ravish all thy beating veins with joy,
Here is a lass of Venus' court, my boy,
Here, gentle shepherd, here's for thee a piece,
The fairest face, the flower of gallant Greece.

VENUS' SHOW.

Enter **HELEN** in her bravery, with **FOUR CUPIDS** attending on her, each having his fan in his hand to fan fresh air in her face: she sings as follows:

Se Diana nel cielo è una stella
Chiara e lucente, piena di splendore,
Che porge luc' all' affanato cuore;
Se Diana nel ferno è una dea
Che da conforto all' anime dannate,
Che per amor son morte desperate;
Se Dian, ch' in terra è delle ninfe
Reina imperativa di dolei fiori,
Tra bosch' e selve da morte a pastori;
Io son un Diana dolce e rara,
Che con li guardi io posso far guerra

A Dian' infern' in cielo, e in terra.

[HELEN exits.

PARIS
Most heavenly dames, was never man as I,
Poor shepherd swain, so happy and unhappy;
The least of these delights that you devise,
Able to wrape and dazzle human eyes.
But since my silence may not pardoned be,
And I appoint which is the fairest she,
Pardon, most sacred dames, sith one, not all,
By Paris' doom must have this golden ball.
Thy beauty, stately Juno dame divine,
That like to Phoebus' golden beams doth shine,
Approves itself to be most excellent;
But that fair face that doth me most content,
Sith fair, fair dames, is neither she nor she,
But she whom I shall fairest deem to be,
That face is hers that hight the Queen of Love,
Whose sweetness doth both gods and creatures move;
And if the fairest face deserve the ball,
Fair Venus, ladies, bears it from ye all.

[Gives the golden ball to **VENUS**.

VENUS
And in this ball doth Venus more delight
Than in her lovely boy fair Cupid's sight.
Come, shepherd, come; sweet Venus is thy friend;
No matter how thou other gods offend.

[**VENUS** takes **PARIS** away with her. Exeunt.

JUNO
But he shall rue and ban the dismal day
Wherein his Venus bare the ball away;
And heaven and earth just witnesses shall be,
I will revenge it on his progeny.

PALLAS
Well, Juno, whether we be lief or loth,
Venus hath got the apple from us both.

[Exeunt.

ACT III

SCENE I

Enter **COLIN**, the enamoured shephered, who sings his passion of love.

COLIN
O gentle Love, ungentle for thy deed,
Thou mak'st my heart
A bloody mark

With piercing shot to bleed!
Shoot soft, sweet Love, for fear thou shoot amiss,
For fear too keen
Thy arrows been,

And hit the heart where my belovèd is.
Too fair that fortune were, nor never I
Shall be so blest,
Among the rest,

That Love shall seize on her by sympathy.
Then since with Love my prayers bear no boot,
This doth remain
To cease my pain,

I take the wound, and die at Venus' foot.

[Exit **COLIN**.

SCENE II

Enter **HOBBINOL**, **DIGGON**, and **THENOT**.

HOBBINOL
Poor Colin, woeful man, thy life forspoke by love,
What uncouth fit, what malady, is this that thou dost prove?

DIGGON
Or Love is void of physic clean, or Love's our common wrack,
That gives us bane to bring us low, and let us medicine lack.

HOBBINOL
That ever Love had reverence 'mong silly shepherd swains!
Belike that humour hurts them most that most might be their pains.

THENOT
Hobbin, it is some other god that cherisheth her sheep,
For sure this Love doth nothing else but make our herdmen weep.

DIGGON
And what a hap is this, I pray, when all our woods rejoice,
For Colin thus to be denied his young and lovely choice?

THENOT
She hight indeed so fresh and fair that well it is for thee,
Colin and kind hath been thy friend, that Cupid could not see.

HOBBINOL
And whither wends yon thriveless swain? like to the stricken deer,
Seeks he dictam[n]um for his wound within our forest here?

DIGGON
He wends to greet the Queen of Love, that in these woods doth won,
With mirthless lays to make complaint to Venus of her son.

THENOT
Ah, Colin, thou art all deceived! she dallies with the boy,
And winks at all his wanton pranks, and thinks thy love a toy.

HOBBINOL
Then leave him to his luckless love, let him abide his fate;
The sore is rankled all too far, our comfort comes too late.

DIGGON
Though Thestylis the scorpion be that breaks his sweet assault,
Yet will Rhamnusia vengeance take on her disdainful fault.

THENOT
Lo, yonder comes the lovely nymph, that in these Ida vales
Plays with Amyntas' lusty boy, and coys him in the dales!

HOBBINOL
Thenot, methinks her cheer is changed, her mirthful looks are laid,
She frolics not; pray god, the lad have not beguiled the maid!

SCENE III

Enter **OENONE** with a wreath of poplar on her head.

OENONE [Aside]
Beguiled, disdained, and out of love! Live long, thou poplar-tree,

And let thy letters grow in length, to witness this with me.
Ah, Venus, but for reverence unto thy sacred name,
To steal a silly maiden's love, I might account it blame!
And if the tales be true I hear, and blush for to recite,
Thou dost me wrong to leave the plains and dally out of sight.
False Paris, this was not thy vow, when thou and I were one,
To range and change old love for new; but now those days be gone.
But I will find the goddess out, that she thy vow may read,
And fill these woods with my laments for thy unhappy deed.

HOBBINOL
So fair a face, so foul a thought to harbour in his breast!
Thy hope consumed, poor nymph, thy hap is worse than all the rest.

OENONE
Ah, shepherds, you bin full of wiles, and whet your wits on books,
And wrape poor maids with pipes and songs, and sweet alluring looks!

DIGGON
Mis-speak not all for his amiss; there bin that keepen flocks,
That never chose but once, nor yet beguilèd love with mocks.

OENONE
False Paris, he is none of those; his trothless double deed
Will hurt a many shepherds else that might go nigh to speed.

THENOT
Poor Colin, that is ill for thee, that art as true in trust
To thy sweet smert as to his nymph Paris hath bin unjust.

OENONE
Ah, well is she hath Colin won, that nill no other love!
And woe is me, my luck is loss, my pains no pity move!

HOBBINOL
Farewell, fair nymph, sith he must heal alone that gave the wound;
There grows no herb of such effect upon Dame Nature's ground.

[Exeunt **HOBBINOL**, **DIGGON**, and **THENOT**.

SCENE IV

Enter **MERCURY** with Vulcan's **CYCLOPS**.

MERCURY
Here is a nymph that sadly sits, and she belike

Can tell some news, Pyracmon, of the jolly swain we seek:
Dare wage my wings, the lass doth love, she looks so bleak and thin;
And 'tis for anger or for grief: but I will talk begin.

OENONE [Aside]
Break out, poor heart, and make complaint, the mountain flocks to move,
What proud repulse and thankless scorn thou hast received of love.

MERCURY
She singeth; sirs, be hushed a while.

[**OENONE** sings as she sits.

OENONE'S COMPLAINT.

Melpomene, the Muse of tragic songs,
With mournful tunes, in stole of dismal hue,
Assist a silly nymph to wail her woe,
And leave thy lusty company behind.
Thou luckless wreath! becomes not me to wear
The poplar-tree for triumph of my love:
Then, as my joy, my pride of love, is left,
Be thou unclothèd of thy lovely green;
And in thy leaves my fortune written be,
And them some gentle wind let blow abroad,
That all the world may see how false of love
False Paris hath to his Oenone been.

[The song ended, **OENONE** sitting still, **MERCURY** speaks.

MERCURY
Good day, fair maid; weary belike with following of your game,
I wish thee cunning at thy will, to spare or strike the same.

OENONE
I thank you, sir; my game is quick, and rids a length of ground,
And yet I am deceived, or else 'a had a deadly wound.

MERCURY
Your hand perhaps did swerve awry.

OENONE
Or else it was my heart.

MERCURY
Then sure 'a plied his footmanship.

OENONE

'A played a ranging part.

MERCURY
You should have given a deeper wound.

OENONE
I could not that for pity.

MERCURY
You should have eyed him better, then.

OENONE
Blind love was not so witty.

MERCURY
Why, tell me, sweet, are you in love?

OENONE
Or would I were not so.

MERCURY
Ye mean because 'a does ye wrong.

OENONE
Perdy, the more my woe.

MERCURY
Why, mean ye Love, or him ye loved?

OENONE
Well may I mean them both.

MERCURY
Is love to blame?

OENONE
The Queen of Love hath made him false his troth.

MERCURY
Mean ye, indeed, the Queen of Love?

OENONE
Even wanton Cupid's dame.

MERCURY
Why, was thy love so lovely, than?

OENONE

His beauty hight his shame;
The fairest shepherd on our green.

MERCURY
Is he a shepherd, than?

OENONE
And sometime kept a bleating flock.

MERCURY
Enough, this is the man.
Where wons he, then?

OENONE
About these woods, far from the poplar-tree.

MERCURY
What poplar mean ye?

OENONE
Witness of the vows betwixt him and me,
And come and wend a little way, and you shall see his skill.

MERCURY
Sirs, tarry you.

OENONE
Nay, let them go.

MERCURY
Nay, not unless you will.
Stay, nymph, and harken what I say of him thou blamest so.
And, credit me, I have a sad discourse to tell thee ere I go.
Know then, my pretty mops, that I hight Mercury,
The messenger of heaven, and hither fly
To seize upon the man whom thou dost love,
To summon him before my father Jove,
To answer matter of great consequence:
And Jove himself will not be long from hence.

OENONE
Sweet Mercury, and have poor Oenone's cries
For Paris' fault y-pierced th' unpartial skies?

MERCURY
The same is he, that jolly shepherd's swain.

OENONE

His flock do graze upon Aurora's plain,
The colour of his coat is lusty green;
That would these eyes of mine had never seen
His 'ticing curlèd hair, his front of ivory,
Then had not I, poor I, bin unhappy.

MERCURY
No marvel, wench, although we cannot find him,
When all too late the Queen of Heaven doth mind him.
But if thou wilt have physic for thy sore,
Mind him who list, remember thou him no more,
And find some other game, and get thee gone;
For here will lusty suitors come anon,
Too hot and lusty for thy dying vein,
Such as ne'er wont to make their suits in vain.

[Exit **MERCURY** with **CYCLOPS**.

OENONE
I will go sit and pine under the poplar-tree,
And write my answer to his vow, that every eye may see.

[Exit.

SCENE V

Enter **VENUS**, **PARIS**, and a company of **SHEPHERDS**.

VENUS
Shepherds, I am content, for this sweet shepherd's sake,
A strange revenge upon the maid and her disdain to take.
Let Colin's corpse be brought in place, and buried in the plain.
And let this be the verse, The love whom Thestylis hath slain.
And, trust me, I will chide my son for partiality,
That gave the swain so deep a wound, and let her scape him by.

1ST SHEPHERD
Alas that ever Love was blind, to shoot so far amiss!

VENUS
Cupid my son was more to blame, the fault not mine, but his.

[Exeunt **SHEPHERDS**.

PARIS
O madam, if yourself would deign the handling of the bow,

Albeit it be a task, yourself more skill, more justice know.

VENUS
Sweet shepherd, didst thou ever love?

PARIS
Lady, a little once.

VENUS
And art thou changed?

PARIS
Fair Queen of Love, I loved not all attonce.

VENUS
Well, wanton, wert thou wounded so deep as some have been,
It were a cunning cure to heal, and rueful to be seen.

PARIS
But tell me, gracious goddess, for a start and false offence,
Hath Venus or her son the power at pleasure to dispense?

VENUS
My boy, I will instruct thee in a piece of poetry,
That haply erst thou hast not heard: in hell there is a tree,
Where once a-day do sleep the souls of false forsworen lovers,
With open hearts; and there about in swarms the number hovers
Of poor forsaken ghosts, whose wings from off this tree do beat
Round drops of fiery Phlegethon to scorch false hearts with heat.
This pain did Venus and her son entreat the prince of hell
T' impose to such as faithless were to such as loved them well:
And, therefore, this, my lovely boy, fair Venus doth advise thee,
Be true and steadfast in thy love, beware thou do disguise thee;
For he that makes but love a jest, when pleaseth him to start,
Shall feel those fiery water-drops consume his faithless heart.

PARIS
Is Venus and her son so full of justice and severity?

VENUS
Pity it were that love should not be linkèd with indifferency.
However lovers can exclaim for hard success in love,
Trust me, some more than common cause that painful hap doth move:
And Cupid's bow is not alone his triumph, but his rod;
Nor is he only but a boy, he hight a mighty god;
And they that do him reverence have reason for the same,
His shafts keep heaven and earth in awe, and shape rewards for shame.

PARIS
And hath he reason to maintain why Colin died for love?

VENUS
Yea, reason good, I warrant thee, in right it might behove.

PARIS
Then be the name of Love adored; his bow is full of might,
His wounds are all but for desert, his laws are all but right.

VENUS
Well, for this once me list apply my speeches to thy sense,
And Thestylis shall feel the pain for Love's supposed offence.

[The **SHEPHERDS** bring in **COLIN'S** hearse, singing.

SHEPHERDS
Welladay, welladay, poor Colin, thou art going to the ground,
The love whom Thestylis hath slain,
Hard heart, fair face, fraught with disdain,
Disdain in love a deadly wound.
Wound her, sweet Love, so deep again,
That she may feel the dying pain
Of this unhappy shepherd's swain.
And die for love as Colin died, as Colin died.

VENUS
Shepherds, abide; let Colin's corpse be witness of the pain
That Thestylis endures in love, a plague for her disdain.
Behold the organ of our wrath, this rusty churl is he;
She dotes on his ill-favoured face, so much accursed is she.

[A foul crooked **CHURL** enters, with **THESTYLIS**, a fair Lass, who woos him, and sings an old song called
"The Wooing of Colman": he crabbedly refuses her, and goes out of place: she tarries behind.

PARIS
Ah, poor unhappy Thestylis, unpitied is thy pain!

VENUS
Her fortune not unlike to hers whom cruël thou hast slain.

[**THESTYLIS** sings and the **SHEPHERDS** reply.

[**THE SONG**.

THESTYLIS
The strange effects of my tormented heart,
Whom cruël love hath woeful prisoner caught,

Whom cruël hate hath into bondage brought,
Whom wit no way of safe escape hath taught,
Enforce me say, in witness of my smart,
There is no pain to foul disdain in hardy suits of love.

SHEPHERDS
There is no pain, &c.

THESTYLIS
Cruël, farewell.

SHEPHERDS
Cruël, farewell.

THESTYLIS
Most cruël thou, of all that nature framed.

SHEPHERDS
Most cruël, &c.

THESTYLIS
To kill thy love with thy disdain.

SHEPHERDS
To kill thy love with thy disdain.

THESTYLIS
Cruël, Disdain, so live thou named.

SHEPHERDS
Cruël, Disdain, &c.

THESTYLIS
And let me die of Iphis' pain.

SHEPHERDS
A life too good for thy disdain.

THESTYLIS
Sith this my stars to me allot,
And thou thy love hast all forgot.

SHEPHERDS
And thou, &c.

[Exit **THESTYLIS**.

[The grace of this song is in the Shepherds' echo to her verse.

VENUS
Now, shepherds, bury Colin's corpse, perfume his hearse with flowers,
And write what justice Venus did amid these woods of yours.

[The **SHEPHERD'S** carry out **COLIN'S** hearse.

How now, how cheers my lovely boy, after this dump of love?

PARIS
Such dumps, sweet lady, as these, are deadly dumps to prove.

VENUS
Cease, shepherd, there are other news, after this melancholy:
My mind presumes some tempest toward upon the speech of Mercury.

SCENE VI

MERCURY with Vulcan's **CYCLOPS** enter.

MERCURY
Fair Lady Venus, let me pardoned be,
That have of long bin well-beloved of thee,
If, as my office bids, myself first brings
To my sweet madam these unwelcome tidings.

VENUS
What news, what tidings, gentle Mercury,
In midst of my delights, to trouble me?

MERCURY
At Juno's suit, Pallas assisting her,
Sith both did join in suit to Jupiter,
Action is entered in the court of heaven;
And me, the swiftest of the planets seven,
With warrant they have thence despatched away,
To apprehend and find the man, they say,
That gave from them that self-same ball of gold,
Which, I presume, I do in place behold;
Which man, unless my marks be taken wide,
Is he that sits so near thy gracious side.
This being so, it rests he go from hence,
Before the gods to answer his offence.

VENUS
What tale is this? doth Juno and her mate

Pursue this shepherd with such deadly hate,
As what was then our general agreement,
To stand unto they nill be now content?
Let Juno jet, and Pallas play her part,
What here I have, I won it by desert;
And heaven and earth shall both confounded be,
Ere wrong in this be done to him or me.

MERCURY
This little fruit, if Mercury can spell,
Will send, I fear, a world of souls to hell.

VENUS
What mean these Cyclops, Mercury? is Vulcan waxed so fine,
To send his chimney-sweepers forth to fetter any friend of mine? –
Abash not, shepherd, at the thing; myself thy bail will be. –
He shall be present at the court of Jove, I warrant thee.

MERCURY
Venus, give me your pledge.

VENUS
My ceston, or my fan, or both?

MERCURY [Taking her fan]
Nay, this shall serve, your word to me as sure as is your oath,
At Diana's bower; and, lady, if my wit or policy
May profit him, for Venus' sake let him make bold with Mercury.

[Exit with the Cyclops.

VENUS
Sweet Paris, whereon dost thou muse?

PARIS
The angry heavens, for this fatal jar,
Name me the instrument of dire and deadly war.

[Exeunt.

ACT IV

SCENE I

Enter one of Diana's **NYMPHS** followed by **VULCAN**.

VULCAN
Why, nymph, what need ye run so fast? What though but black I be?
I have more pretty knacks to please than every eye doth see;
And though I go not so upright, and though I am a smith,
To make me gracious you may have some other thing therewith.

SCENE II

Enter **BACCHUS**.

BACCHUS
Yee Vulcan, will ye so indeed? – Nay, turn, and tell him, trull,
He hath a mistress of his own to take his bellyfull.

VULCAN
Why, sir, if Phoebe's dainty nymphs please lusty Vulcan's tooth,
Why may not Vulcan tread awry as well as Venus doth?

NYMPH
Ye shall not taint your troth for me: you wot it very well,
All that be Dian's maids are vowed to halter apes in hell.

BACCHUS
I' faith, I' faith, my gentle mops, but I do know a cast,
Lead apes who list, that we would help t' unhalter them as fast.

NYMPH
Fie, fie, your skill is wondrous great! had thought the God of Wine
Had tended but his tubs and grapes, and not ben half so fine.

VULCAN
Gramercy for that quirk, my girl

BACCHUS
That's one of dainty's frumps.

NYMPH
I pray, sir, take't with all amiss; our cunning comes by lumps.

VULCAN
Sh'ath capped his answer in the Q.

NYMPH
How says 'a, has she so?
As well as she that capped your head to keep you warm below.

VULCAN
Yea, then you will be curst I see.

BACCHUS
Best let her even alone.

NYMPH
Yea, gentle gods, and find some other string to harp upon.

BACCHUS
Some other string! agreed, i'faith, some other pretty thing;
'Twere shame fair maids should idle be: how say you, will ye sing?

NYMPH
Some rounds or merry roundelays, we sing no other songs;
Your melancholic notes not to our country mirth belongs.

VULCAN
Here comes a crew will help us trim.

SCENE III

Enter **MERCURY** with the **CYCLOPS**.

MERCURY
Yea, now our task is done.

BACCHUS
Then, merry Mercury; more than time this round were well begun.

[They sing "Hey down, down, down," &c.

[The song done, the **NYMPH** winds a horn in **VULCAN'S** ear, and runs out.

VULCAN
A harlotry, I warrant her.

BACCHUS
A peevish elvish shroe.

MERCURY
Have seen as far to come as near, for all her ranging so.
But, Bacchus, time well-spent I wot, our sacred father Jove,
With Phoebus and the God of War are met in Dian's grove.

VULCAN

Then we are here before them yet: but stay, the earth doth swell;
God Neptune, too, (this hap is good,) doth meet the Prince of Hell.

[**PLUTO** ascends from below in his chair;

[**NEPTUNE** enters at another way.

PLUTO
What jars are these, that call the gods of heaven and hell below?

NEPTUNE
It is a work of wit and toil to rule a lusty shroe.

SCENE IV

Enter **JUPITER**, **SATURN**, **APOLLO**, **MARS**, **JUNO**, **PALLAS**, and **DIANA**.

JUPITER
Bring forth the man of Troy, that he may hear
Whereof he is to be arraignèd here.

NEPTUNE
Lo, where 'a comes, prepared to plead his case,
Under condúct of lovely Venus grace!

[Enter **VENUS** with **PARIS**.

MERCURY
I have not seen a more alluring boy.

APOLLO
So beauty hight the wreck of Priam's Troy.

[The **GODS** being set in Diana's bower; **JUNO**, **PALLAS**, **VENUS**, and **PARIS** stand on sides before them.

VENUS
Lo, sacred Jove, at Juno's proud complaint,
As erst I gave my pledge to Mercury,
I bring the man whom he did late attaint,
To answer his indictment orderly;
And crave this grace of this immortal senate,
That ye allow the man his advocate.

PALLAS
That may not be; the laws of heaven deny
A man to plead or answer by attorney.

VENUS
Pallas, thy doom is all too péremptory.

APOLLO
Venus, that favour is denied him flatly:
He is a man, and therefore by our laws,
Himself, without his aid, must plead his cause.

VENUS
Then 'bash not, shepherd, in so good a case;
And friends thou hast, as well as foes, in place.

JUNO
Why, Mercury, why do ye not indict him?

VENUS
Soft, gentle Juno, I pray you, do not bite him.

JUNO
Nay, gods, I trow, you are like to have great silence,
Unless this parrot be commanded hence.

JUPITER
Venus, forbear, be still. – Speak, Mercury.

VENUS
If Juno jangle, Venus will reply.

MERCURY
Paris, king Priam's son, thou art arraigned of partiality.
Of sentence partial and unjust; for that without indifferency,
Beyond desert or merit far, as thine accusers say,
From them, to Lady Venus here, thou gavest the prize away:
What is thine answer?

[**PARIS'** oration to the Council of the **GODS**.

PARIS
Sacred and just, thou great and dreadful Jove,
And you thrice-reverend powers, whom love nor hate
May wrest awry; if this, to me a man,
This fortune fatal be, that I must plead
For safe excusal of my guiltless thought,
The honour more makes my mishap the less.
That I a man must plead before the gods,
Gracious forbearers of the world's amiss,
For her, whose beauty how it hath enticed,

This heavenly senate may with me aver.
But sith nor that nor this may do me boot,
And for myself myself must speaker be,
A mortal man amidst this heavenly presence;
Let me not shape a long defence to them
That ben beholders of my guiltless thoughts.
Then for the deed, that I may not deny,
Wherein consists the full of mine offence,
I did upon command; if then I erred,
I did no more than to a man belonged.
And if, in verdit of their forms divine,
My dazzled eye did swarve or surfeit more
On Venus' face than any face of theirs,
It was no partial fault, but fault of his,
Belike, whose eyesight not so perfect was
As might discern the brightness of the rest.
And if it were permitted unto men,
Ye gods, to parlè with your secret thoughts,
There ben that sit upon that sacred seat,
That would with Paris err in Venus' praise.
But let me cease to speak of error here;
Sith what my hand, the organ of my heart,
Did give with good agreement of mine eye,
My tongue is vowed with process to maintain.

PLUTO
A jolly shepherd, wise and eloquent.

PARIS
First, then, arraigned of partiality,
Paris replies, "Unguilty of the fact";
His reason is, because he knew no more
Fair Venus' ceston than Dame Juno's mace,
Nor never saw wise Pallas' crystal shield.
Then as I looked, I loved and liked attonce,
And as it was referred from them to me,
To give the prize to her whose beauty best
My fancy did commend, so did I praise
And judge as might my dazzled eye discern.

NEPTUNE
A piece of art, that cunningly, pardie,
Refers the blame to weakness of his eye.

PARIS
Now, for I must add reason for my deed,
Why Venus rather pleased me of the three;
First, in the intrails of my mortal ears,

The question standing upon beauty's blaze,
The name of her that hight the Queen of Love,
Methought, in beauty should not be excelled.
Had it been destinèd to majesty
(Yet will I not rob Venus of her grace),
Then stately Juno might have borne the ball.
Had it to wisdom been intitulèd,
My human wit had given it Pallas then.
But sith unto the fairest of the three
That power, that threw it for my farther ill,
Did dedicate this ball; and safest durst
My shepherd's skill adventure, as I thought,
To judge of form and beauty rather than
Of Juno's state or Pallas' worthiness,
That learned to ken the fairest of the flock,
And praisèd beauty but by nature's aim;
Behold, to Venus Paris gave this fruit,
A daysman chosen there by full consent,
And heavenly powers should not repent their deeds.
Where it is said, beyond desert of hers
I honoured Venus with this golden prize,
Ye gods, alas, what can a mortal man
Discern betwixt the sacred gifts of heaven?
Or, if I may with reverence reason thus;
Suppose I gave, and judged corruptly then,
For hope of that that best did please my thought,
This apple not for beauty's praise alone;
I might offend, sith I was pardonèd,
And tempted more than ever creature was
With wealth, with beauty, and with chivalry,
And so preferred beauty before them all,
The thing that hath enchanted heaven itself.
And for the one, contentment is my wealth;
A shell of salt will serve a shepherd swain,
A slender banquet in a homely scrip,
And water running from the silver spring.
For arms, they dread no foes that sit so low;
A thorn can keep the wind from off my back,
A sheep-cote thatched a shepherd's palace hight.
Of tragic Muses shepherds con no skill;
Enough is them, if Cupid ben displeased,
To sing his praise on slender oaten pipe.
And thus, thrice-reverend, have I told my tale,
And crave the torment of my guiltless soul
To be measúrèd by my faultless thought.
If warlike Pallas or the Queen of Heaven
Sue to reverse my sentence by appeal,
Be it as please your majesties divine;

The wrong, the hurt, not mine, if any be,
But hers whose beauty claimed the prize of me.
Paris having ended, Jupiter speaks.

JUPITER
Venus, withdraw your shepherd for a space.
Till he again be called for into place.

[Exeunt **VENUS** and **PARIS**.

Juno, what will ye after this reply,
But doom with sentence of indifferency?
And if you will but justice in the cause.
The man must quited be by heaven's laws.

JUNO
Yea, gentle Jove, when Juno's suits are moved,
Then heaven may see how well she is beloved.

APOLLO
But, madam, fits it majesty divine
In any sort from justice to decline?

PALLAS
Whether the man be guilty, yea or no,
That doth not hinder our appeal, I trow.

JUNO
Phoebus, I wot, amid this heavenly crew,
There be that have to say as well as you.

APOLLO
And, Juno, I with them, and they with me,
In law and right must needfully agree.

PALLAS
I grant ye may agree, but be content
To doubt upon regard of your agreement.

PLUTO
And if ye marked, the man in his defence
Said thereof as 'a might with reverence.

VULCAN
And did ye very well, I promise ye.

JUNO
No doubt, sir, you could note it cunningly.

SATURN
Well, Juno, if ye will appeal, ye may.
But first despatch the shepherd hence away.

MARS
Then Vulcan's dame is like to have the wrong.

JUNO
And that in passion doth to Mars belong.

JUPITER
Call Venus and the shepherd in again.

[Exit **MERCURY**.

BACCHUS
And rid the man that he may know his pain.

APOLLO
His pain, his pain, his never-dying pain,
A cause to make a many more complain.

[**MERCURY** brings in **VENUS** and **PARIS**.

JUPITER
Shepherd, thou hast ben heard with equity and law,
And for thy stars do thee to other calling draw,
We here dismiss thee hence, by order of our senate:
Go take thy way to Troy, and there abide thy fate.

VENUS
Sweet shepherd, with such luck in love, while thou dost live,
As may the Queen of Love to any lover give.

PARIS
My luck is loss, howe'er my love do speed:
I fear me Paris shall but rue his deed.

[Exit **PARIS**.

APOLLO
From Ida woods now wends the shepherd's boy,
That in his bosom carries fire to Troy.

JUPITER
Venus, these ladies do appeal, you see.
And that they may appeal the gods agree:

It resteth, then, that you be well content
To stand in this unto our final judgment;
And if King Priam's son did well in this,
The law of heaven will not lead amiss.

VENUS
But, sacred Jupiter, might thy daughter choose,
She might with reason this appeal refuse:
Yet, if they be unmovèd in their shames,
Be it a stain and blemish to their names;
A deed, too, far unworthy of the place,
Unworthy Pallas' lance or Juno's mace;
And if to beauty it bequeathèd be,
I doubt not but it will return to me.
She lays down the ball.

PALLAS
Venus, there is no more ado than so,
It resteth where the gods do it bestow.

NEPTUNE
But, ladies, under favour of your rage,
Howe'er it be, you play upon the vantage.

JUPITER
Then, dames, that we more freely may debate,
And hear th' indifferent sentence of this senate,
Withdraw you from this presence for a space,
Till we have throughly questioned of the case:
Dian shall be your guide; nor shall you need
Yourselves t' inquire how things do here succeed;
We will, as we resolve, give you to know,
By general doom how everything doth go.

DIANA
Thy will, my wish. – Fair ladies, will ye wend?

JUNO
Beshrew her whom this sentence doth offend.

VENUS
Now, Jove, be just; and, gods, you that be Venus' friends,
If you have ever done her wrong, then may you make amends.

[Exeunt **DIANA**, **JUNO**, **PALLAS**, and **VENUS**.

JUPITER
Venus is fair, Pallas and Juno too.

VULCAN

But tell me now without some more ado,
Who is the fairest she, and do not flatter.

PLUTO

Vulcan, upon comparison hangs all the matter:
That done, the quarrel and the strife were ended.

MARS

Because 'tis known, the quarrel is pretended.

VULCAN

Mars, you have reason for your speech, perdy;
My dame, I trow, is fairest in your eye.

MARS

Or, Vulcan, I should do her double wrong.

SATURN

About a toy we tarry here so long.
Give it by voices, voices give the odds;
A trifle so to trouble all the gods!

NEPTUNE

Believe me, Saturn, be it so for me.

BACCHUS

For me.

PLUTO

For me.

MARS

For me, if Jove agree.

MERCURY

And, gentle gods, I am indifferent;
But then I know who's likely to be shent.

APOLLO

Thrice-reverend gods, and thou, immortal Jove,
If Phoebus may, as him doth much behove.
Be licensèd, according to our laws.
To speak uprightly in this doubted cause,
(Sith women's wits work men's unceasing woes),
To make them friends, that now bin friendless foes,
And peace to keep with them, with us, and all,

That make their title to this golden ball;
(Nor think, ye gods, my speech doth derogate
From sacred power of this immortal senate;)
Refer this sentence where it doth belong:
In this, say I, fair Phoebe hath the wrong;
Not that I mean her beauty bears the prize
But that the holy law of heaven denies
One god to meddle in another's power;
And this befell so near Diana's bower,
As for th' appeasing this unpleasant grudge,
In my conceit, she hight the fittest judge.
If Jove comptrol not Pluto's hell with charms,
If Mars have sovereign power to manage arms,
If Bacchus bear no rule in Neptune sea,
Nor Vulcan's fire doth Saturn's scythe obey,
Suppress not, then, 'gainst law and equity,
Diana's power in her own territory,
Whose regiment, amid her sacred bowers,
As proper hight as any rule of yours.
Well may we so wipe all the speech away,
That Pallas, Juno, Venus, hath to say,
And answer that, by justice of our laws
We were not suffered to conclude the cause.
And this to me most egal doom appears,
A woman to be judge among her feres.

MERCURY
Apollo hath found out the only mean
To rid the blame from us and trouble clean.

VULCAN
We are beholding to his sacred wit.

JUPITER
I can commend and well allow of it;
And so derive the matter from us all,
That Dian have the giving of the ball.

VULCAN
So Jove may clearly excuse him in the case,
Where Juno else would chide and brawl apace.

[They **ALL** rise.

MERCURY
And now it were some cunning to divine
To whom Diana will this prize resign.

VULCAN
Sufficeth me, it shall be none of mine.

BACCHUS
Vulcan, though thou be black, thou'rt nothing fine.

VULCAN
Go bathe thee, Bacchus, in a tub of wine;
The ball's as likely to be mine as thine.

[Exeunt.

ACT V

SCENE I

Enter **DIANA, JUNO, PALLAS, VENUS**.

DIANA
Lo, ladies, far beyond my hope and will, you see,
This thankless office is imposed to me;
Wherein if you will rest as well content,
As Dian will be judge indifferent,
My egal doom shall none of you offend,
And of this quarrel make a final end:
And therefore, whether you be lief or loath,
Confirm your promise with some sacred oath.

PALLAS
Phoebe, chief mistress of this sylvan chace,
Whom gods have chosen to conclude the case,
That yet in balance undecided lies,
Touching bestowing of this golden prize,
I give my promise and mine oath withal,
By Styx, by heaven's power imperial,
By all that 'longs to Pallas' deity,
Her shield, her lance, ensigns of chivalry,
Her sacred wreath of olive and of bay,
Her crested helm, and else what Pallas may,
That wheresoe'er this ball of purest gold,
That chaste Diana here in hand doth hold,
Unpartially her wisdom shall bestow,
Without mislike or quarrel any mo,
Pallas shall rest content and satisfied,
And say the best desert doth there abide.

JUNO

And here I promise and protest withal,
By Styx, by heaven's power imperial,
By all that 'longs to Juno's deity,
Her crown, her mace, ensigns of majesty,
Her spotless marriage-rites, her league divine,
And by that holy name of Proserpine,
That wheresoe'er this ball of purest gold,
That chaste Diana here in hand doth hold,
Unpartially her wisdom shall bestow.
Without mislike or quarrel any mo,
Juno shall rest content and satisfied,
And say the best desert doth there abide.

VENUS

And, lovely Phoebe, for I know thy doom
Will be no other than shall thee become,
Behold, I take thy dainty hand to kiss,
And with my solemn oath confirm my promise,
By Styx, by Jove's immortal empery,
By Cupid's bow, by Venus' myrtle-tree,
By Vulcan's gift, my ceston and my fan.
By this red rose, whose colour first began
When erst my wanton boy (the more his blame)
Did draw his bow awry and hurt his dame,
By all the honour and the sacrifice
That from Cithaeron and from Paphos rise,
That wheresoe'er this ball of purest gold,
That chaste Diana here in hand doth hold,
Unpartially her wisdom shall bestow,
Without mislike or quarrel any mo,
Venus shall rest content and satisfied,
And say the best desert doth there abide.

[**DIANA** describes the Nymph Eliza, a figure of the **QUEEN**.

DIANA

It is enough, and, goddesses, attend.
There wons within these pleasant shady woods,
Where neither storm nor sun's distemperature
Have power to hurt by cruël heat or cold,
Under the climate of the mild heaven;
Where seldom lights Jove's angry thunderbolt,
For favour of that sovereign earthly peer;
Where whistling winds make music 'mong the trees, –
Far from disturbance of our country gods,
Amids the cypress-springs, a gracious nymph,
That honour Dian for her chastity,

And likes the labours well of Phoebe's groves;
The place Elyzium hight, and of the place
Her name that governs there Eliza is;
A kingdom that may well compare with mine,
An ancient seat of kings, a second Troy,
Y-compassed round with a commodious sea:
Her people are y-clepèed Angeli,
Or, if I miss, a letter is the most:
She giveth laws of justice and of peace;
And on her head, as fits her fortune best,
She wears a wreath of laurel, gold, and palm;
Her robes of purple and of scarlet dye;
Her veil of white, as best befits a maid:
Her ancestors live in the House of Fame:
She giveth arms of happy victory,
And flowers to deck her lions crowned with gold.
This peerless nymph, whom heaven and earth belove,
This paragon this only, this is she,
In whom do meet so many gifts in one,
On whom our country gods so often gaze,
In honour of whose name the Muses sing;
In state Queen Juno's peer, for power in arms
And virtues of the mind Minerva's mate,
As fair and lovely as the Queen of Love,
As chaste as Dian in her chaste desires:
The same is she, if Phoebe do no wrong,
To whom this ball in merit doth belong.

PALLAS
If this be she whom some Zabeta call,
To whom thy wisdom well bequeaths the ball,
I can remember, at her day of birth,
How Flora with her flowers strewed the earth,
How every power with heavenly majesty
In person honoured that solemnity.

JUNO
The lovely Graces were not far away,
They threw their balm for triumph of the day.

VENUS
The Fates against their kind began a cheerful song,
And vowed her life with favour to prolong.
Then first gan Cupid's eyesight wexen dim;
Belike Eliza's beauty blinded him.
To this fair nymph, not earthly, but divine,
Contents it me my honour to resign.

PALLAS
To this fair queen, so beautiful and wise,
Pallas bequeaths her title in the prize.

JUNO
To her whom Juno's looks so well become.
The Queen of Heaven yields at Phoebe's doom;
And glad I am Diana found the art,
Without offence so well to please desert.

DIANA
Then mark my tale. The usual time is nigh,
When wont the Dames of Life and Destiny,
In robes of cheerful colours, to repair
To this renownèd queen so wise and fair,
With pleasaunt songs this peerless nymph to greet;
Clotho lays down her distaff at her feet,
And Lachesis doth pull the thread at length,
The third with favour gives it stuff and strength,
And for contráry kind affords her leave,
As her best likes, her web of life to weave.
This time we will attend, and in the mean while
With some sweet song the tediousness beguile.

[The Music sounds, and the **NYMPHS** within sing or solfa with voices and instruments awhile.

[Then enter **CLOTHO**, **LACHESIS**, and **ATROPOS**, singing as follows: the state being in place.

[**THE SONG**.

CLOTHO
Humanae vitae filum sic volvere Parcae.

LACHESIS
Humanae vitae filum sic tendere Parcae.

ATROPOS
Humanae vitae filum sic scindere Parcae.

CLOTHO
Clotho colum bajulat.

LACHESIS
Lachesis trahit.

ATROPOS
Atropos occat.
Tres simul. Vive diu foelix votis hominúmque deúmque,

Corpore, mente, libro, doctissima, candida, casta.

[They lay down their properties at the Queen's feet.

CLOTHO
Clotho colum pedibus.

LACHESIS
Lachesis tibi pendula fila.

ATROPOS
Et fatale tuis manibus ferrum Atropos offert.
Tres simul. Vive diu felix, &c.

[The song being ended, **CLOTHO** speaks to the **QUEEN**.

CLOTHO
Gracious and wise, fair Queen of rare renown,
Whom heaven and earth belove, amid thy train,
Noble and lovely peers, to honour thee,
And do thee favour more than may belong
By nature's law to any earthly wight,
Behold continuance of our yearly due;
Th' unpartial Dames of Destiny we meet,
As have the gods and we agreed in one,
In reverence of Eliza's noble name;
And humbly, lo, her distaff Clotho yields!

LACHESIS
Her spindle Lachesis, and her fatal reel,
Lays down in reverence at Eliza's feet
Te tamen in terris unam tria numina Divam
Invita statuunt natura lege sorores,
Et tibi non aliis didicerunt parcere Parcoe.

ATROPOS
Dame Atropos, according as her feres,
To thee, fair Queen, resigns her fatal knife:
Live long the noble phoenix of our age,
Our fair Eliza, our Zabeta fair!

DIANA
And, lo, beside this rare solemnity,
And sacrifice these dames are wont to do,
A favour, far indeed contráry kind,
Bequeathèd is unto thy worthiness
This prize from heaven and heavenly goddesses!

[She delivers the ball of gold to the **QUEEN'S** own hands.

Accept it, then, thy due by Dian's doom.
Praise of the wisdom, beauty, and the state,
That best becomes thy peerless excellency.

VENUS
So, fair Eliza, Venus doth resign
The honour of this honour to be thine.

JUNO
So is the Queen of Heaven content likewise
To yield to thee her title in the prize.

PARIS
So Pallas yields the praise hereof to thee.
For wisdom, princely state, and peerless beauty.

EPILOGUS

Omnes simul. Vive diu felix votis hominumque deumque,
Corpore, mente, libro, doctissima, candida, casta,

[Exeunt **OMNES**.